For Julie-Anne
❖ J M ❖

For Vladan
❖ J W ❖

First published 1999 by Walker Books Ltd
87 Vauxhall Walk, London SE11 5HJ

2 4 6 8 10 9 7 5 3 1

Text © 1999 Jan Mark

Illustrations © 1999 Juan Wijngaard

This book has been typeset in
Leawood Book, Monotype Centaur and Zapf Renaissance.

Printed in Hong Kong/China

British Library Cataloguing in Publication Data
A catalogue record for this book is
available from the British Library.

ISBN 0-7445-5511-6

THE MIDAS TOUCH
JAN MARK

ILLUSTRATED BY
JUAN WIJNGAARD

WALKER BOOKS
AND SUBSIDIARIES
LONDON · BOSTON · SYDNEY

Nowadays people are people, from head to foot. We come in all shapes, colours and sizes but you know where you are with people. If you look at a goat you think, that is a goat. If you look at a tree you think, that is a tree. If you look at a person you think, this is a person.

Things were not always so simple. Long ago, when the world was still finding its feet, there lived creatures you would never see today. Deep in the woods lived men who were half-goats, and they were called satyrs. There were men who were half-horses and they were called centaurs. There were girls who were half-trees and they were called hamadryads. They followed the god Dionysus, and humans kept out of their way. Such creatures could be dangerous.

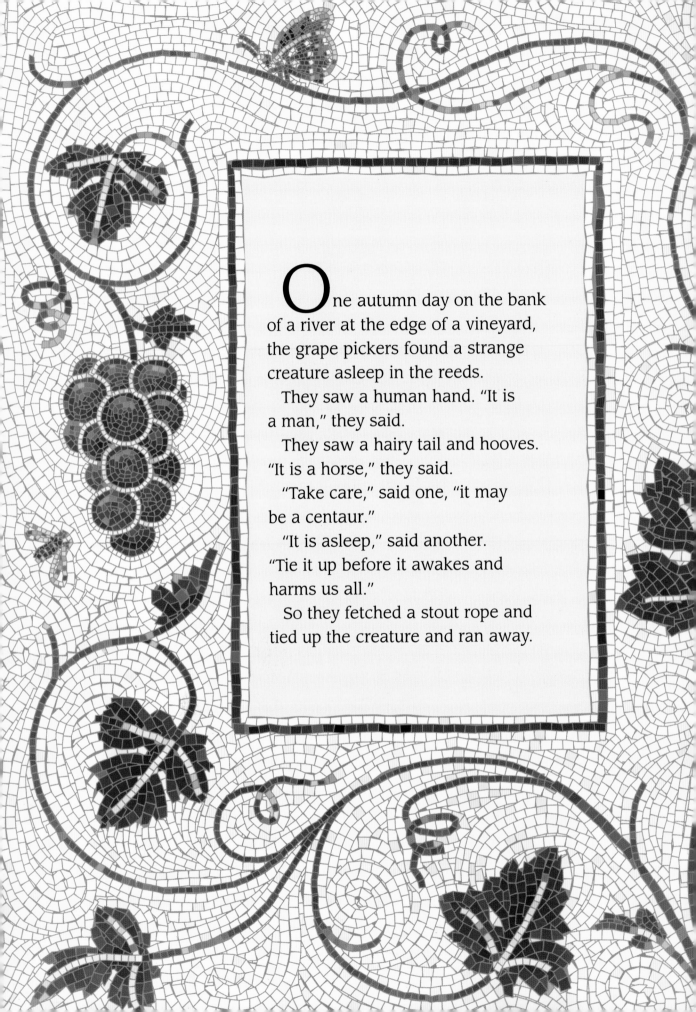

One autumn day on the bank of a river at the edge of a vineyard, the grape pickers found a strange creature asleep in the reeds.

They saw a human hand. "It is a man," they said.

They saw a hairy tail and hooves. "It is a horse," they said.

"Take care," said one, "it may be a centaur."

"It is asleep," said another. "Tie it up before it awakes and harms us all."

So they fetched a stout rope and tied up the creature and ran away.

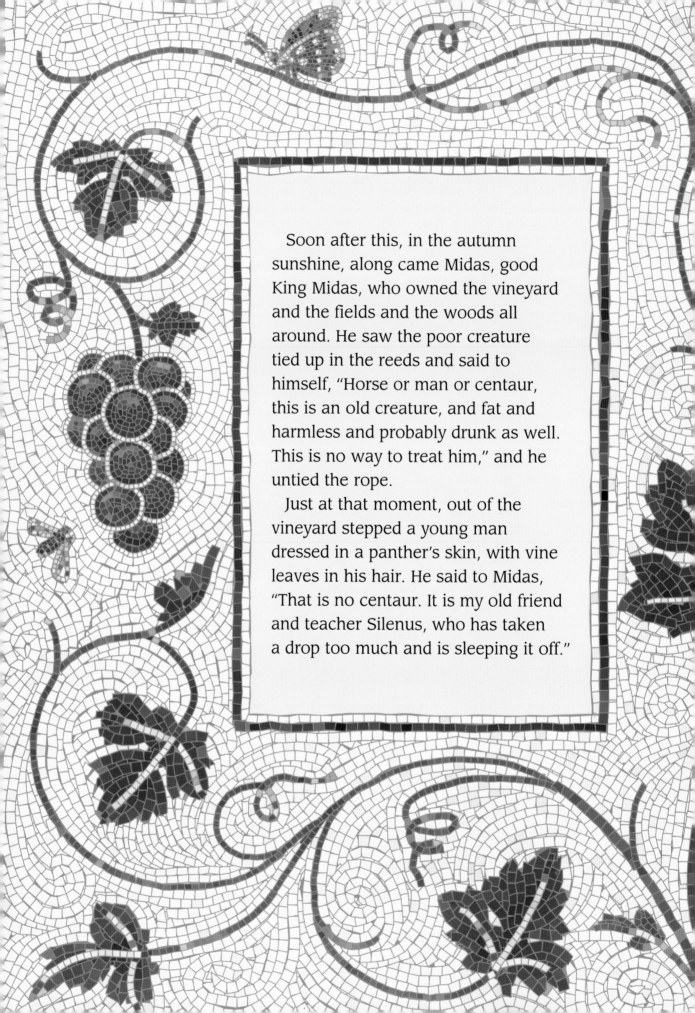

Soon after this, in the autumn sunshine, along came Midas, good King Midas, who owned the vineyard and the fields and the woods all around. He saw the poor creature tied up in the reeds and said to himself, "Horse or man or centaur, this is an old creature, and fat and harmless and probably drunk as well. This is no way to treat him," and he untied the rope.

Just at that moment, out of the vineyard stepped a young man dressed in a panther's skin, with vine leaves in his hair. He said to Midas, "That is no centaur. It is my old friend and teacher Silenus, who has taken a drop too much and is sleeping it off."

Now Midas, though mortal himself, was the son of a goddess and he knew a god when he saw one. So he bowed low when the young man said, "I am Dionysus, and for your kindness to this foolish old person, I will give you a reward. You have only to name it."

Midas was good and Midas was wise, but the gods can drive a man mad if they have a mind to do it. Midas asked for something that he did not need and had not wanted until that mad moment. He said to Dionysus, "Let everything that I touch be turned to gold."

Dionysus smiled a terrible smile. He did not say: *Everything?* He did not say: *Are you sure?* He did not say: *Think about it.* He only said, "My pleasure," and he meant it.

"In the morning," said Dionysus, "when you wake, the golden touch shall be yours. Everything that you touch will be turned to gold."

Then Midas bowed again and when he looked up Dionysus had gone, taking drunken old Silenus with him.

Midas walked home through the vineyard, touching the grapes with his finger and thinking: Tomorrow, everything that I touch with this finger will turn to gold.

And Dionysus, far away in the woods, knew his thought and smiled his terrible smile and whispered, "But who said anything about your finger?"

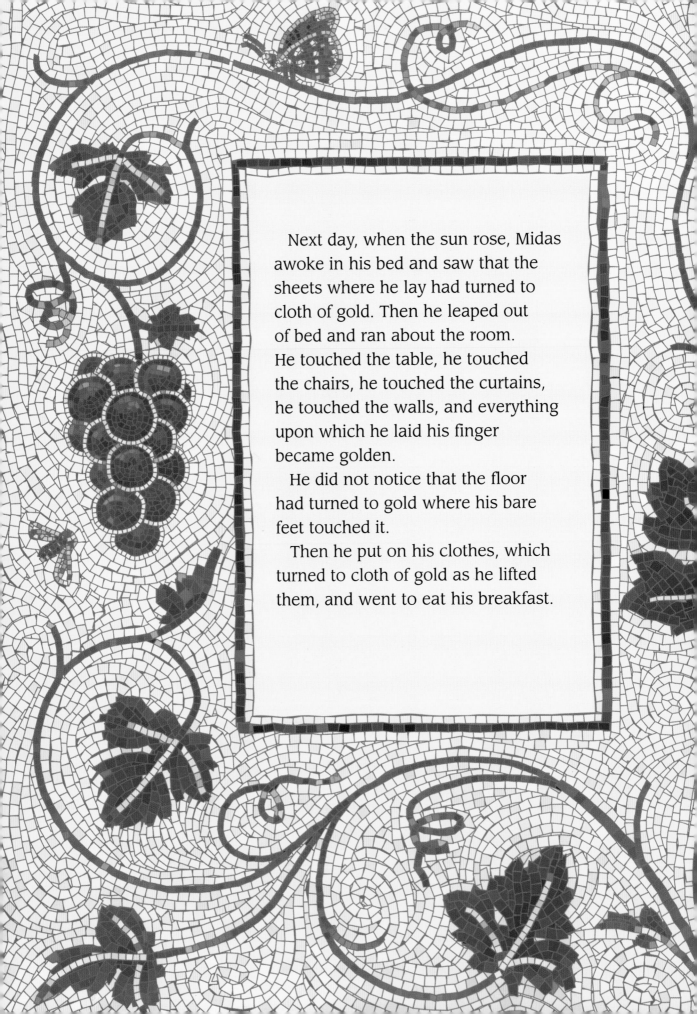

Next day, when the sun rose, Midas awoke in his bed and saw that the sheets where he lay had turned to cloth of gold. Then he leaped out of bed and ran about the room. He touched the table, he touched the chairs, he touched the curtains, he touched the walls, and everything upon which he laid his finger became golden.

He did not notice that the floor had turned to gold where his bare feet touched it.

Then he put on his clothes, which turned to cloth of gold as he lifted them, and went to eat his breakfast.

There on the table before him lay a plate of baked fish, a basket of new hot loaves and a flagon of wine with a goblet to drink from. But before he began to eat he touched the basket, the plate, the flagon and the goblet, and all turned to gold as he did so. Then he lifted his knife to cut the bread; and then he touched the bread.

The knife would not cut. The soft hot bread was hard and yellow.

"Fool," said Midas to himself. "The knife is gold and so is the bread, where I touched them. I must take more care." So he picked up a spoon, which turned to gold, and lifted a fish from the plate. He put it into his mouth and bit it, and felt cold, hard metal between his teeth.

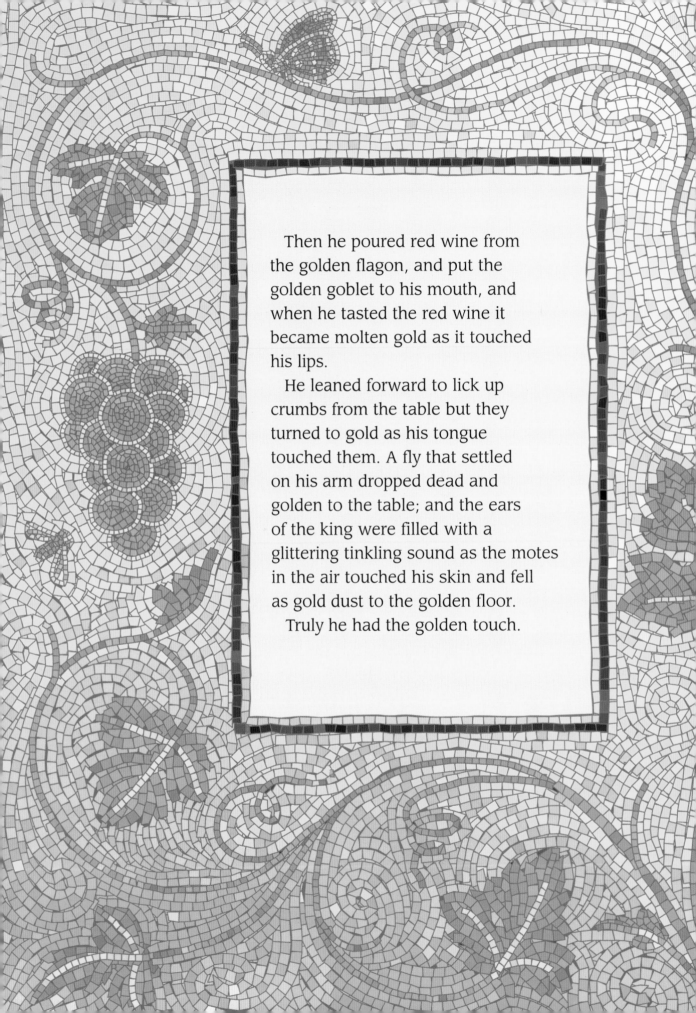

Then he poured red wine from the golden flagon, and put the golden goblet to his mouth, and when he tasted the red wine it became molten gold as it touched his lips.

He leaned forward to lick up crumbs from the table but they turned to gold as his tongue touched them. A fly that settled on his arm dropped dead and golden to the table; and the ears of the king were filled with a glittering tinkling sound as the motes in the air touched his skin and fell as gold dust to the golden floor.

Truly he had the golden touch.

Everything that King Midas touched, or that touched him, was turned to gold, and in a few days he would be dead of starvation in the midst of the greatest fortune man had ever seen. Even the earth would turn to gold where he lay buried.

Then he beat his head and tore his hair and ran howling through the palace and across the gardens, into the vineyard, and everything that he touched fell lifeless behind him. The grass turned to gold beneath his feet. The bunches of grapes that had hung plump and purple yesterday chimed like bells, and above all rang the maddening tinkle of falling golden dust.

Then the king heard another sound through the ringing and jingling and chiming. Someone was laughing. Midas stopped still and there before him stood the young man in the panther skin, with the vine leaves around his head, smiling his terrible smile.

"Well, Midas," said Dionysus, "and how do you like the golden touch?"

Midas fell on his face before the god and screamed, "Take it away! Take it away!"

Dionysus said, "But Midas, I gave you exactly what you wished for."

Midas looked up at the god and he looked at the smile and he said, "I was mad to wish for it. I beg you to take it away."

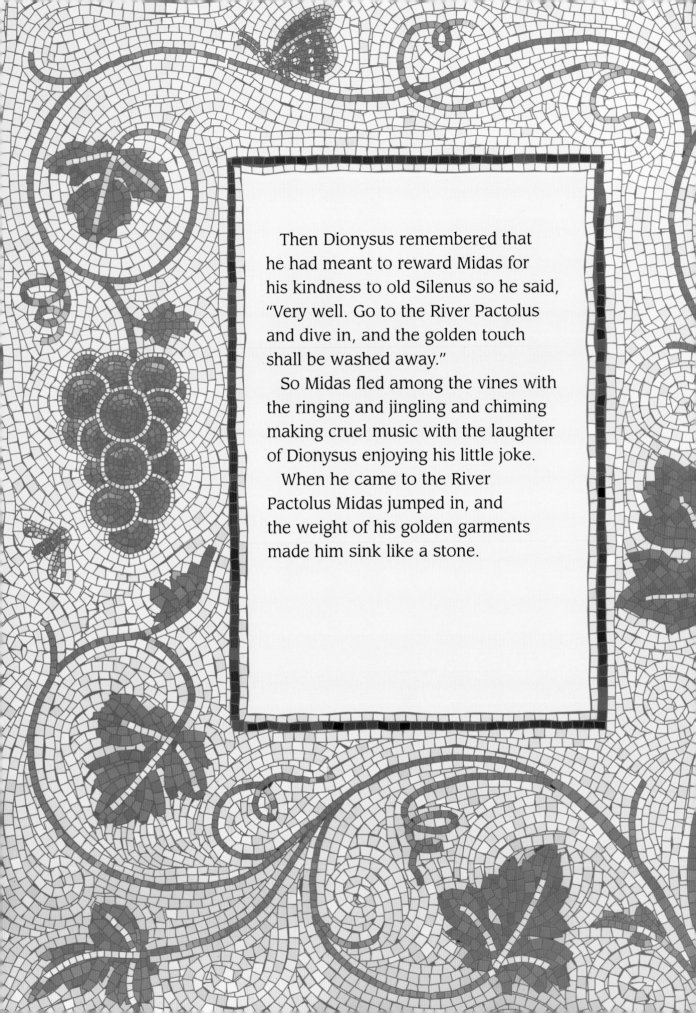

Then Dionysus remembered that he had meant to reward Midas for his kindness to old Silenus so he said, "Very well. Go to the River Pactolus and dive in, and the golden touch shall be washed away."

So Midas fled among the vines with the ringing and jingling and chiming making cruel music with the laughter of Dionysus enjoying his little joke.

When he came to the River Pactolus Midas jumped in, and the weight of his golden garments made him sink like a stone.

But as he touched the river-bed, and the water closed over his head, he opened his eyes and saw his golden robes turn white and soft and light as linen; he drifted to the surface leaving the golden touch behind.

He ran home, drenched, through the vineyard, plucking grapes from the vines and eating them as he went, and all he heard was the song of the birds and the wind in the trees.

But the sands of the River Pactolus were golden for ever more.